DYING A LITTLE

DYING A LITTLE
BARRY DEMPSTER

Wolsak & Wynn

© Barry Dempster, 2011

No part of this publication may be reproduced, stored in a retrieval system or transmitted, in any form or by any means, without the prior written consent of the publisher or a license from The Canadian Copyright Licensing Agency (Access Copyright). For an Access Copyright license, visit www.accesscopyright.ca or call toll free to 1-800-893-5777.

Cover image: "Fire Horse" by Natalie Waldburger
Author's photograph: DMN Photo Art
Cover Design: Leigh Kotsilidis
Typset in Charlemagne Std & Bembo
Printed by Coach House Books Toronto, Canada

The publisher gratefully acknowledges the support of the Canada Council for the Arts, the Ontario Arts Council and the Canada Book Fund.

Wolsak and Wynn Publishers Ltd.
#102–69 Hughson Street North
Hamilton, ON
Canada L8R 1G5

Library and Archives Canada Cataloguing in Publication

Dempster, Barry, 1952-
    Dying a little / Barry Dempster.

Poems.
ISBN 978-1-894987-58-5

    I. Title.

PS8557.E4827D95 2011   C811'.54   C2011-905950-9

For Karen

and Cathy and Andrew

Each substance of a grief hath twenty shadows.
					William Shakespeare, *Richard II*

CONTENTS

13	SHRINE
14	HEADLINE: *DYING WITHOUT A WILL CAN BE DEVASTATING*
16	THE LOVING KINGDOM OF TERMITES
17	FLEETING
18	MALE BONDING
20	MACABRE
21	NUDES
24	SORROW, A REPRISE
25	DYING A LITTLE
26	TEARS OF JOY
28	CHILDHOOD STORY
30	RESEMBLANCES
32	DOUBLE 1: DEAD MAN
34	DREAM TIME
36	BLISS
38	THE ROAR, A MID-LIFE POEM
39	BODY PARTS
42	VIEWS FROM AN ILLNESS
44	DRIVE 1: DISTANT
46	EGO SURGERY
48	BIG MISTAKE
50	HEADACHE
52	EXPLORATORY SURGERY
54	88 DECEMBERS
55	GET LOST
57	DOUBLE 2: PERFECT STRANGER
59	RAPTURE
60	DRIVE 2: RISK
62	AS LUCK WOULD HAVE IT
64	PLYMOUTH SUNDANCE
66	MOSQUITO CONTROL
68	SAY SO
69	HEAVEN-BENT
71	GIVING AWAY THE GARDEN
73	DEVIL DEATH

75	FIX ME
77	TULIPS
79	YOU ARE SURROUNDED BY MUSIC
80	BONFIRE
81	CONCERT HALL, THE CARLU
83	PERENNIAL
85	THURSDAY CRUEL
87	BUILDING STAIRS
88	THE MAPLES ARE BLEEDING
89	WHERE DOES IT HURT?
91	THE WHOLE OF IT
93	EVERYTHING IS GOING TO BE FINE
95	DEATH DATE
99	ACKNOWLEDGEMENTS

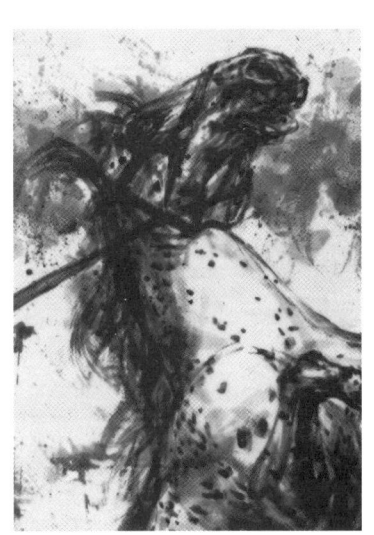

SHRINE

You come to the vase of carnations, bury
        your nose in the pink and white frills.
Your dead mother's favourite flower.
        Still? Seven years of conversing
with silence, time enough for your
        body to shed all its cells, for her to fall
in love with delphiniums, or plain old roses.

Mother's shrine takes up one corner
        of your already crowded heart:
a reliquary of bananas and brown sugar,
        a Billy Graham tract, a faith
in blouses that can be worn untucked.
        And, of course, God, perched
on her left breast like a rhinestone brooch
        (how she liked to fiddle with him, twist
his gleam). Apparently, seven years
        of death haven't changed her a bit.

And so you pretend to stay the same,
        despite your new cells, telling yourself,
mother is just around the corner,
        people-watching as always, her hairdo
in place, her pink skirt matching
        her pink sweater. On days when your
skin crawls with the thoughts of another
        seven silences, you think of heaven
peeled from its flowery clouds
        like the shock of a familiar face.

HEADLINE: *DYING WITHOUT A WILL, CAN BE DEVASTATING*

Innovate, is all he can think of
here in law land, sad-assed,
slumped in a wobbly chair.
Dreaming up his own death,
distributing his worldly mediocrities.
Not a masochist after all, in fact
a surprising love for himself.
Suddenly, the scratch of his signature
blossoms into an ornate tattoo.

The lawyer coughs then apologizes,
as if the two sounds were a dancing
brother act: St. Peter and his twin, Cerberus.
The assistant attached to her screen
by a mess of wires
types with the monotony of the undead.
There's no way he's dying
in such a drab, tasteless manner.
He thinks of leaving his fingers
to the secretarial pool, his eyes
to the back of someone's previously
unimportant head.

Imagine: *The Will, an Opera*,
Don Giovanni tussling with a paper devil,
libretto by Villon,
scrunched-up soul torn to shreds.
To his dead mother, he leaves
all childhood memories, the shape
of a sandcastle towering for a few hours
at the edge of the sea.
And to his imaginary brother, a loss
far greater than either can imagine.

To the stranger whose eye he caught
twenty years ago on a train,
he leaves all possibilities.
The rest goes to his reincarnation
fund, the first fresh face
who has the sense to ask,
What's in it for me?

THE LOVING KINGDOM OF TERMITES

Halfway to complete collapse,
porches sagging, septic tank
backed up, window screens taped
with band-aids. Family cottage
pissed at the great beyond
for not taking it along. Who knew
roofs and railings could suffer so?

And you, surviving son, gill-
green with grief, sicking hammers
and brooms on every crack.
The past will live again! Future
a slick new coat of paint.

The moment is crust,
a dust-cloak of grey
in the loving kingdom of termites.
Bury your sobs in a sneeze.
Disintegrating slowly
your only hope.

FLEETING

The white-on-its-way-to-yellow cat lies rolled
like a Russian hat in a corner of the pet store.
Oh, kitty, you say, *my heart is a mouse,
a skitter of plucked nerves*. But the cat
just lies there, rippleless, snoring, oblivious
to the blue twitch in the long alley of your wrist.

You are also nothing but a squint to the clerk
who sells you clip-ons, a mere symptom
to the pharmacist who bundles your tube of secrets
in a plain white bag. Akin to invisible;
even the breeze of a page being flipped
has more existence than this.

On the car radio, a litany of love songs,
no mention of you. So why feel
so overexposed, so stripped, bathed in
a cheesy pink light that takes years off
your lack of faith? You'd think everyone
had succumbed to desire, all
the roadside daisies ripped and bald.

You wheel into your driveway, finally alone
with your omissions, engine ticking
as it cools, mouse surrendering to a trap.
The impatiens in the front flower bed
wilting, words organizing themselves
into Things to Do. It turns out
your life doesn't love you after all,
the voice on your answering machine
apologizing for never being home.

MALE BONDING

Let's open up, he says,
arms hula hoop wide,
well on their way to a hug.
A blink later, we'll be
bonding, telling tales of
threesomes and guilty
pop culture pleasures,
things that chip away
at our hardy hearts
without cracking the shells.
Then we'll be brothers –
a photo op – men
who have gone beyond
the goalpost, the comb-over,
the homoerotic.
Let's open up and see
whose tears can dribble
fastest. Before we know it,
we'll be comparing fathers,
how well we learned to read
those moustache twitches,
how suavely we learned
to hate ourselves.
Of course, we'll swear
we're nothing like Roy or Ted,
and will love our own sons
even when they carry us
to our final beds.
Let's roll up our sleeves,
let's get our hands dirty,
let's put our balls
on the table. Let's open
a bottle that *pops*
instead of *whooshes*, and believe
in the possibility
of love without genes

or sex. When I enter the hug,
all is bone and leaking heat,
a familiar wall.
If I were to whisper in his ear,
would I finally hear
what I've been trying to say?
Let's sing, let's shrug our shoulders,
let's pull down our pants.
We can do this, we're heroes,
we're he-men. Here is
the sheer finale
where the truth finally
emerges like a rabbit
pulled from a baseball cap.
Am I holding on to him,
or is he holding on
to me, a chip
of heartwood protruding
from what used to be a fist?

MACABRE

"*A* is for Amy who trips on a crutch, *B* is for Barry who feels too much."

Languishing on Edward Gorey's Yarmouth Port couch,
a raccoon coat tucked around your cold ankles,
a coterie of ghostly cats doing their utmost
to look Egyptian. This is illness on a bristly
Thursday afternoon, immersed in the absurd, a house
full of beached stones and dead children. Are you in love
with death, or just deathly afraid? Strange how you can't tell
the difference. A skinny boy's legs stick out
of a smothering carpet and you laugh yourself silly.
A blonde fright wig of a girl crash-landing on a steep
stairwell, *hardy har*. The broken man inside you
suddenly beside himself. Shivering, you clamor
to your feet and do the proper tour, the bloodstained
calendars, the grisly stuffed toys. While just outside,
a gaping mouthful of tombstones bleach the grass.
It's almost nightmare, some dream boundary
crossed after too much dessert. Until slowly,
it all starts to feel normal, even your own hideousness,
a limit tipped upside down, all the terrors
spilling out. One more shudder and you're hobbling
for the exit where the huge rare magnolia
is so real it's fake. Is that the Eastham Sea
you smell or just the scent of long life rotting?
A part of you will die today and you can't stop giggling.

NUDES

1/

This is the body that shocked him with its nakedness,
page 267, no-one's lucky number; in a film catalogue,
a story about Mexico and politics, a picture of a young
woman, nude from mid-torso up, her skin the colour
of coffee with the milk still dissolving, her arms pressed
tightly, uncomfortably, to her sides, her breasts,
nipples shiny, uneven, the left one fuller, more enticing.
She is, of course, asleep and available, a combination
that tells him more about himself than he cares to decipher,
her dreadlocks splayed out on the pillowless sheets
like unlit torches. Her mouth is turned to the right,
beyond him, yet whispering, he swears, about middle-aged men,
how they mistake experience for wisdom, desire for truth.

2/

Mother took to her nightgown the minute he was born,
handing him the fast-fading warmth of a sterilized bottle.
It wasn't until he was ten and secretive as a folded cuff
that he saw her flesh again, in a forest thicket where she'd gone
to pee, squatting in a sea of vinca, her ass almost touching
the waxy green as if it too had grown there, a wild mushroom
so white it would have shrieked if someone had reached to pluck it.
When her eyes met his, animal eyes welled with misunderstanding,
she became a blur, a scramble of blue woollen slacks and dead leaves.

3/

The only part of his father's body he noticed as a child
was his penis, thick and horsey, cosmically hairy.
Otherwise he was armless, bellyless, toeless, a ghost stunt.
Years later, rushing him to the hospital, the ambulance
spinning with bleeds of brownish light, his knees and fingernails
were much too bright. Were there hairs growing from that nose,
he didn't know, or which teeth were false, or how many moles
parading across those shoulders? All he recognized was the dangle
of that old penis, like a muscle cut from a rippling thigh;
bigger than his, the usual fatherly lack of generosity.

4/

For a time, he was disappointed, sex and its expectations
of superhuman lusciousness, bodies shaped in butter,
then dipped in gold. His first lover had muffins for breasts,
the next was knobby kneecaps from the waist down.
After months of simmering lust and a blowout of fantasies,
a pimple gleamed from a rather scalded-looking bum.
So much imperfection, a haze one shade away
from a blotch. He had almost given up, but then he met her,
flipped over her wrist to find a nakedness
of tiny blue canals. He'd never thought to look beyond
the obvious before, the secret of metaphor.

5/

He keeps looking, can't help himself, the word *nude*
like a unicorn sighting. The way a new friend manages
to achieve both lithesome and doughy in the same stark chest.
Or ankle bones suddenly gone slinky on a perch of fuck-me shoes.
Or that tan space between lifted T-shirt and faded jeans,
where his hand could easily have an accident. Glimpses
of intimacy: bits of colour, pinks and mauves, swirling
in a tempest of freckles; a shadow pointing to a deeper shadow;
a curve where bone suddenly becomes the soft curl of a stream.

6/

It ends with him stepping from the shower, slapped silly
by the steamy mirror that insists on seeing nothing
but a fence of ribs, tucks and blemishes galore, a pair
of sucked-in hips and an afterthought of legs that just go
on and on. More naked than nude, overexposed,
those sprung coils of useless intent. Wait until he gets his hands
on this. He wipes clean the mirror, a wide swathe
of self-abnegation. *We're still here*, the nerves
in his groin cry out in high-hoped voices.

SORROW, A REPRISE

Again last night it scratched on your door,
willing to wear away its flesh
for the honour of haunting you, of
sneaking in through your pores and filling you
with hopelessness, the kind of fumes
roses produce one moment before they die.

No way were you going to participate;
your masochistic days done.
You lay there, a pillow stuffed with
happiness between your knees, biting
the numbness from your tongue, refusing
to grip that doorknob, that ball of pain.

Wrapped in sweaty sheets,
you shoved your earplugs deeper.
The scratching continued – long,
lacquered fingernails.
And beneath the noise, a whisper
seeping through the cracks, promising

the sort of self-indulgence
men used to get arrested for.
You end up under the bed, holding
fast to a maze of screws and springs.
Scratch, scratch, scratch.
No way you're ever going vertical again,
tears pouring down your chin like movie rain.

Sorrow kept scraping
until you were splinters.
Come morning, you crawled for the door,
naked as a scrape. Nothing there
but nerve and muscle
face down in a hole of bones.

DYING A LITTLE

Sunset was a fireball that evening, obliterating
the paddock, turning fences into spears of
plunged light. It was all I could do not to burst
into flames as I stretched for my wife's shadow.
I was thinking a lot about my wife, talking
as we were about another wife, sweetest Cathy,
whose joy of a breast, burst into a homemade bomb
of cancer cells, had now *metastasized*, a word
tied in too many places with barbs and moans.
We were sliding our tongues into cavities of hope,
telling tales of minor miracles, toying with the light.
And then we just sat there on the back deck,
word junkies on a crash, dogs sniffing at our empty
wineglasses. Down at the barn, the horses
softly snorted, great black angels shaking
their huge, insistent heads. Farther away,
a thread of wolf lament led us towards grief.
My wife's death is far more frightening
than my own, let's face it, an abandonment.
Then my friends' deaths, one by one, matches
squeezed in fingertips, worm-like wraiths of ash.
The world dying, orange and crimson,
like those disaster films where body counts
are beautiful, where death proves itself a genius
of the inconsolable. There was much to be afraid of
that sunset: Cathy with embers glowing in her chest,
a wife who stood on the edge unable to tell
the difference between a smolder and a hand.
Slowly we brought the conversation back to life,
lit candles against the steady stream of moths,
refilled our glasses. But none of this could change
the fact that we'd all died a little tonight,
that our fingertips had leaked into pools of tinny light,
trickling between the deck's gaps.
Later, our high beams would slam into midnight
as we spun the country driveway, trying to outrun
those horses that were dying to ride us home.

TEARS OF JOY

We're crying when kettles boil,
crying when the razor coaxes
soft whiskers from our chins, when
the families on commercials
get happier for pennies a day.

Such a shock when things work out, when
floods aren't washing us away or
fire shrinking our too-thin skins.
We woke up this morning and were
still in love, our wives brushing

their lush coiffures, our cats playing
with pieces of string, their new best friends.
All is well, the midnight bell, no begging
bowls or ripe red sirens, no pleading shots
of men's hands outstretched or women with

baby-like bundles clutched to their breasts.
Celebrations instead of
telethons, smiles gleaming like
tambourines. Except for us, of course,
we're still crying, cereal boxes

almost full, a chorus line of
comfortable shoes in our closets,
an argument we're sure to win.
Joy so rare, it's a major
reunion, an airport swimming in tears.

We're crying as fridges hum because
we've heard the silences and felt
the lack of cool when wounds start
festering. We're crying for
the squirrels and their cheeks of nuts, their

memories of hollowness. Crying
to the beat of our own hearts,
the persistence of it all, no
matter the cracks and bleeds. Sitting here,
watching words go where they couldn't have

yesterday, we can't stop weeping luck,
dollops of the silvery stuff.
We're crying all the way through
tomorrow when the world
is sure to start ending again.

CHILDHOOD STORY

Dad's was the one where Grammie
beckoned him to her bed, breathing toy words
like *babe* and *darlin'*, only to grab him
by the hair and yank until the roots
split, screaming it was all his fault,
whatever had beached her like this,
broken, whatever had gone wrong
with her brain. He claimed
this was why he went bald at 19.
Why love was so beaten and bruised
he mistook it for a casualty.

88 years with his battered spiel;
red string firecrackers
snapping on sidewalks.
Most of the time his face
unreadable: staring holes in things.
When I reached the age of dissent,
he began telling the story,
excusing himself from fatherhood,
burrowing deeper into a lonesomeness
no-one could share.

But then the blessing of senility,
memories bitmapping: great
peaceful squares. He began focussing
on my dead mother, how she'd saved
his life with her perfect disposition.
Next, my wife, the best daughter-in-law
a man with so many scars could have.
I was halfway through a swallow
the night he added *and a perfect son*,
lucky not to choke.

Now that he's gone, he's reaching out.
Dreams of losing a little version
of my hand in his, the hairs on his knuckles
tufting like shivers. Just yesterday,
he followed me to the dentist.
I lay there in that torture chair, eyes
fisted, trying to banish awareness
to my fingertips. There was his grip again,
a big furry mitt, squeezing away the fear.

Now that he's free of memory,
he no longer has to skulk. He can come
when he's called, smooth the sheets
to perfection, lay a palm over the broken bits,
warm them whole again. He holds me
to the bottom of that aching root,
that writhing. Leaves me calmer
than I was before, revelling
in a love no longer unrequited.

RESEMBLANCES

Too close to be recognized,
Too deep to grasp,
Too easy to believe.
– Gampopa

Lots of evidence: long hands and short fingers,
flesh pale as cream poured straight from the fridge,

a shyness doubling as charm: the genetic
equivalent of rhymes. And how about

Sundee, Mondee, Tuesdee, etc., the Irish in us,
tongues punched into patterns like those

old computer cards. Uncle Russell's smile
folded in with the dress-up clothes, all the cousins

taking turns in the mirror. The struck matches of
Aunt Lillian's eyes passed around on a windy

night. No wonder we love each other, cunning
narcissists that we are. Sometimes we go too far,

reincarnated Claudius or Cleopatra, former
versions of ourselves. This gold wafer

of an earlobe, these star-shaped moles
on our hips, proof we're never utterly alone.

Not to mention our imaginary friends
who in the same blue shirts are dead

ringers. The neighbours, features morphing
through peepholes in the fence. And what

about that otherwise stranger in Starbucks,
ordering a hot chocolate, our tongues

licking bottom lips in unison?
The Family of Man echoes from the past,

cracked-open smiles and long blue sleeves.
Like Picasso and his little cubist look-alikes.

DOUBLE 1: DEAD MAN

The dead man inside you is eating
half your carrot cake, his pale tongue
ferrying away a dollop of
orange icing, a cinnamon sprinkle
of crumbs. And here you thought his hunger
was only for things he couldn't have:
world peace, self-esteem, true love.
All this time he's been pilfering you
at parties, snatching key facts from your stories,
borrowing whole moments, crafting them
into his own memories. So unlike
what a dead man is supposed to do:
lie there and look bored.
That's the only reason you've let him
stay – the pity quotient, and the fact that
without him there'd be too much space
for yoga/movies/books to fill.

The dead man sneaks up on you
when the lights are killed and the bed
wraps your skeleton like someone
else's arms. At first, it's enough to just
sense him, his slightly fungus smell,
his iceberg subtleties. But then
one of your fingers slithers across the sheet
and disappears in a pool of collarbone.
And before you can mutter *Dear Life*,
you're sliding from your own cool into
the fire that fear has always been.

No surprise to wake up in the morning
dead as well. Cramps and
stuck eyelids. Doomed to scrape
across the day, squash some breath.
You drag one another through a shower,
a hairbrush, a tragedy. Death – a life
you can no longer call your own. You
pack a poison lunch, threaten the clouds
with your measly umbrella. Are these
your legs or his? Does it matter?

DREAM TIME

Remember how he insisted that you
listen to his dreams, the ones where he
wrestled the albino monkeys or scaled
the sheer granite cliff,
heralding adventures he'd never
have thought up on his own.
He especially loved flying naked
over a field of flashlight beams, all
sleek and dangle, his arms
assuming the Superman pose.
Or coming back to life, leaping
to his feet and launching
into something between a jig
and a spasm. He can't get
enough of his dream self,
Morpheus on a slow drip
straight to the hole in his heart.

For him, your eternal brother,
dreams are a place where you can
both be dead, freed from the miles
and misunderstandings, the
egos and bones. Once, you stroked
the blackness of his beard
and every kink was a minnow
darting between the rushing tide
of your fingers. You can do
anything when you're together
like this: ride the tigers, rip
the sickles from the stars,
rearrange your body parts
into rockets, Mars or bust.

All you want to do some days
is sleep, deep in the distance
of his reassuring arms.

You miss him, all of him, even
the him who lives next door.
You miss the knack of really being
here, that sky's-the-limit rush.
You miss his timelessness,
his true names, the flexibility
of the undefined, the little
shivers that singe the hairs
on your arms, surprise, surprise.
Tonight, logic drugged, you're
taking him to Wonderland,
Oz, Never-Never, be prepared.
Eight uninterrupted hours
of deepest sleep, of
monkeys and mystical beards.

BLISS

50 years of wedded bliss, boasts
the invitation, church bells
with their deafening hyperbole.

25 calendars ourselves,
don't we believe in happily-
ever-after? Aren't these
smiles on our faces as we kiss
the old bride, as we pump the groom's hand?

No doubts about love,
hell, we'd even go as far as fate
before it starts sharing spit
with destiny. But bliss, that sizzle
on a grill, that swoon of an expiry date?
50 years of the stuff, a daily snort;
it's a wonder they still have noses.

When our anniversary arrives
in its gold-paper chariot, we'll announce
bliss was now and then –
you remember it well,
a tight black thrill.

Happiness, delight, delectation,
we've had moments with them all,
from full-dress balls
to transfiguring quickies
behind the chimney.

But we're proclaiming misery
too, the hole in the hall
the shape of your foot. Come help us
celebrate the misunderstandings,
the muck. Here comes jealousy
in clothes we can't fit into anymore.

When our 50th materializes,
we'll be dropping crumbs into
our wineglasses, weeping as our lives
PowerPoint past our dimming eyes.
We'll kiss all sorts of smiles, not
knowing if they believe in us or not.

THE ROAR, A MID-LIFE POEM

Hey, you, wind in a monster mask,
I call your bluff. What are you going to do,
swoop me up and throw me across the room?
All you can manage is to clatter
a few windowpanes, boo down the flue,
stir up some long-standing dust.
And maybe a tremble or two
as if someone had left a bone door open,
a worm-wriggled draft.

I'm still okay when you knock the power out,
a lodgepole pine lying on the road
a few crucial feet from my dandy
of a blue spruce. Come on, most of this
is bluster. You aren't really ripping
the starlings, that's just acrobatics.
And the maple you're stripping was already
well on its way to naked.

The hours howl by and my nerves
sputter. My cat does her version
of a cartoon alarm clock
complete with retractable eyes.
By midnight, cold and black,
I've skewered gravity, my legs
in a prickled sleep, my brain
a NASCAR track. Will you never
shut up with all your violence and grief?
Too much of anything is torture.
I swallow the last piece of stale air,
toss my neck into a spasm
and scream *I've had enough!*
into a swirl of ruined leaves.

BODY PARTS

The logic bomb is a killer:
crazed cells with malignant minds,
clocks timed to the last wrinkle.
One minute you're trumping green,
a bursting tautness,
the next you've hunkered down
an inch or two, folds hiding
secrets on the back of your neck.
What used to be a fountain
has become a well, deep reserves
of will and the frailty of wisdom.
Bang, a leg explodes into a crutch.
No chance of a clue in this swollen
nest of veins. A strange old man
wears you, sleeves turned inside out.

★

Here is a picture of you as ovum,
pink and undecided, seconds before
the screeching of sperm, the abacus brigade.
Once upon a time you were ageless,
a cartoon myth. Pre-penetration,
before the membrane popped
and both swimmer and sea sank
like a hard-boiled egg.

★

You're genuine chalk talk, a walking
graph. Spurts of bone, growing out
of your clothes so fast it's obscene.
Stress marks of acne, alien tufts,
pheromones stirring in dark kettles.
15, 16, the numbers feel grubby, touched
too often, too much. You are coming

in your dreams, no boundaries between,
just scratched-up sheets
and drifty humpings of dead skin.

★

Remote control, that fleeting ease
when your body parts are in love
with each another, when your own finger
fits perfectly between your lips,
when your thighs pour you into gravity.
These days you fall backwards into mirrors,
trusting a pair of silver arms
you can't even see.

★

For your 40th, you go hiking
in the Balkan Mountains, learning
that a rock is a rock no matter where.
41st finds you up to your eyebrows
in coral reefs as pink as ripe peaches.
42nd is still in the planning stages, something
to do with mid-air. As long as you're
hurting, as long as muscle groups are sculpting
new maps. For weeks now, you've happily
been a bone spur, your heel aching
with live pride. Still showing, still
thriving, heart waved in a red flag.

★

Too late to study Mandarin, your brain
crimping. Forget The Boston Marathon,
calves full of jellyfish. Mid-life crazy,
yearning for blonde amnesia, for a secret
rendezvous with a former what-the-hell.
Notches on your ass.

Hair tribes hiding out in your ears.
How long before your cock is demoted
to a penis? If only you'd taken the time
to calculate, to shift from tendon to spirit.
There's the old man again,
stuffing his hands into socks.

★

It will be a shock discovering
that your soul has always been
a magpie, mostly mimicry
and lusting after shiny, supple things.
Won't be hard at all to let your body go,
just a shrug, finally claiming a use
for those overrated shoulders. And so
you'll fly with the idea of wings
rather than trying to resurrect
a flesh memory, a fling of arms.
You'll leave behind your nest of voices,
the cock songs and eyebrow hymns,
the sailed scales that a new kid
will mistake for everything that counts.

VIEWS FROM AN ILLNESS

It's like being in a toy sub (you
have the gift for making yourself
small) on the bottom of a bathtub,
a washcloth floating above you
like a floppy black cloud. The water
slipping from tepid to cool, but
only leaking in a little, a prickle
of damp slowly softening to sponge.
Your ears popping, the bubbly sound
that puffballs make when poked
by drops of rain.

Never sure where to find
yourself. The pillowcase an obvious
choice, though you rarely succumb
to the easy. Once, swigging down fever
with a bottle of Evian, you caught
your own reflection just before the swallow.
And, of course, the TV set,
you're always doing cameos
on the dead screen, white-lipped and
belligerent. In a tissue box, there you are,
several layers deep, a grain of relief
at the soul of a painkiller, the password
in a *Get Well* card – that rhyming way
you've always secretly described yourself.

Visiting your parents in the cemetery, you
stroke the tombstone moss, each spore
a different memory. When your mother died
she was poured into a bedside vase;
you took home her rings and things
feeling lost until, throwing away the roses,
you saw her smile curling against your wrist.
They're everywhere, the sick ones
who failed you the way you're

beginning to fail yourself. A thumbprint
in the greasy corner of a snapshot, cancer,
circa 1961. The smell of frayed thread
in an old sewing basket. The teeth marks
on the stem of your father's sucked-dry pipe.

It's a miracle you notice anything, you
and your symptoms scrawled tight
in a goodbye note, wrapped up
in the bleak of a blanket, shell-shocked
in a drop of water sliding dead-end
from a bathtub tap. You're as narrow
as a glance, a sip, a peep. A sliver
of glass pressed under the skin, one
rousing bead of blood. If the covers
suddenly unravelled, pyjama buttons leaping
from their tiny slots, pink flesh dimming
its double glow, what would be left of you?
Perhaps a shiver, a smudge, a scent
of roses rehearsing their final fall.

DRIVE 1: DISTANT

Interminable highway, like a Mafia
promise: she'll never sleep safely again.
Dear destination, go ahead, guess
how much of her will have dropped off
by the end, rolled into a ditch and died.
She is always in between, or so it
seems, arrival one-upping her sad
attempts at speed, weaving
the flickering risks of a white line.

It's that same locked-up feeling
when she reaches for the phone,
unable to steer the distance straight
and Sunday-like. Each ring
ripples into a silence she can't even
hope to fill, disturbing god-knows-what.
The voice on the answering machine
might as well be Martian,
apologies from all the great unknowns.

Who knew distance was such an epidemic.
Even with someone right in front of her,
all she's really touching is the sleeve
of a blue sweater or the feverish gold
of a wedding ring. Long ago she realized
naked was just transparent tape, the heart
still sealed inside. A string of kisses
nothing more than dots lighting up
a map of somewhere she's never been.

Always starting over, remembering
to shut the lights, fill the tank,
take that closed door with her.
One of these days, racing down the highway,
holding a cellphone to her cheek,
she'll suddenly forget where she's going,
or why she wanted to. Miles
between impulse and act, tires spinning,
brain cells a fuss of gravel and dirt.
Travel is tired of itself. If only
she knew the way to regret,
or that rumour of a shortcut to faith.
But distance is the only home she has.

EGO SURGERY

What a shock: that man in the mirror
with the crooked teeth
and sleepless stains beneath his eyes
belongs to me, my responsibility
to feed him chocolate and cheese,
the little luxuries, to keep him squeaky
clean and listen to his poor-me poems,
to love him when the lights are handed in
for the night, when fear puts on
its suit of skin and bone.
When I ask the barber for a trim,
it's true I'm wishing he'd replace my face,
something neat and smiley
from the obit page of *People* magazine
(the sexiest dead or alive).
I snatch the scissors – one
determined muscle, one crunchy snip.
Ego surgery, toss those flaws to a second
chance, keep hope going strong.
I'll be able to love me better,
selfless speaks in such persuasive tones.

Later that same existence, my brother-in-law
and I trade desires, shallow-flipping
through a movie magazine, confessing
that we both find Angelina
a tad grotesque, that Scarlett
is looking chubby, the baby fat issue
getting old, that Nicole still wins
the silky skin award hands down.
We're striving not to be sexist,
and there are certainly no mirrors around.
But all I can feel is flesh, more flesh,
a fruit market of only the sweetest
body parts: plummy cheeks, fat
raspberry nipples, melon-sugary

collarbones. How easy it is to love
the beautiful, or not, the indulgence
of taking it or leaving. And as for us,
two middle-aged guys whose names
might as well both be Wayne,
what are we inspiring as we ravage
our way through the photo gallery?
Would Nicole overlook the blotches
where we've touched ourselves too often,
our sweaty upper lips, our palms
tattooed with magazine ink? Or would she be
too busy staring at a mirror to even notice?

BIG MISTAKE

January, usually so demure
in its white sultan sheets,
has had too much to grieve this year,
tossing back its head, choking
on rain. Today it's wearing a paste
of leftover leaves and what looks like slush
well on the way to some other chemistry.
Faded Christmas wreaths dangle from
dented screen doors. Everywhere,
the plunge of melt disappearing
into sewers. A rake lying across
a brown lawn, fingers curled.

This is the state of things when we hear
Cathy may only have weeks to live,
brain cells scrambling with
tiny fingertip tumours. Mother Nature
on a sci-fi rattle, sorry one time
too many for all the stupid loss,
and stupid it is, this
fumbling fate, this big mistake:
poisonous mushrooms
growing on the undersides
of her shadow, getting bigger
than her flickering bits of self.

We can't imagine her paling
in a hospital bed, head and shoulders
cranked up for that final appearance.
Can't, or won't – amounts to the same
refusal. Instead, we picture her strong enough
to walk these January streets, a red scarf
wrapped around her pretty neck.
We make her stop every now and then
to push a tulip bulb back

into the warming dirt, *not quite,*
not yet. She's kicking at the leaves,
such long, optimistic legs.

The rain persists as we race out to our cars,
doing its damnedest to erase us.
The daring secret is no longer Cathy's
death, but the burst of glow as car doors
open and the overhead lights splash on.
There she is, in our passenger seats,
begging a ride out of this long month,
to a place where the sun is still god
and the snow is in full bloom. We'll take her
anywhere, we realize, outdriving
the downpour, willing to go further
than the truth, that last niggling boundary.

HEADACHE

The sick days keep creeping
as do the grimy telephone calls
trying to trick you into new windows,
new carpets, new ways of disguising old.
Sometimes even love seems to be selling
the idea of a relationship.
The aggression gives you
headaches, like busy signals
bored into the shelves of your brain.
Mostly, you want to lie here, plywood-flimsy,
tracing the exact network of arteries
flinging pain. Such a complex
son of a bitch, no wonder you
disassociate. If you had your druthers
you'd be someone else, someone who
can't speak this faltering language.

But you're a trooper – *forward march*,
off your ass and into yoga class
where the teacher hands out neck massages
as rewards. Later, you'll shop for cat food,
buy gas, all the necessities. You'll be a headache
all day, but won't let it get in the way
of the oldies station, all those rigor mortis
melodies. Long ago you learned to keep
loneliness to yourself.

Back home, back answering the phone:
a subscription to *Time*, an offer
you can hardly refuse. What promises you're
tempted to make, what futures. But it whittles
down to just the headache and you, playing
with a bag of tiny finishing nails.
Exquisite, this existential max,
days when it feels good to be in pain –
a good old-time relationship.

Feed that cat, feel disgruntled
with all existing windows and carpets,
wait for the next fate to call.

EXPLORATORY SURGERY

for Andrew Held

It's those blue, papery slippers
that do the trick, lift my heart
from the tool shelf and set it
in motion, the great fix-'em-all.
I was okay with the flowery
gown and the knots strained across
your spine, fine with the IV line,
the sunken needle and that one
dried drop of blood. I was even
coping with the gurney, wondering
if I could steal you for a ride,
hospital ceiling racing the light.

Throughout the day, your father and I
don't mention knives or staples,
or the possibility of never
seeing you again. Instead,
he reminisces about that
far-off Normandy beach, how
shrapnel dug into the heaps
of sand around him, buried
memories that have since lost
their thud, making it difficult
to tell the difference between
a Spielberg scene and his own youth.
I prop your bag of street clothes
between us, talk around you, leaning
on the puffy fold of your winter coat.

Death files through the hours,
naming itself *melanoma*,
a pretty word that wouldn't be
out of place in the latest
lavish issue of Oprah's magazine,
a treat from Tuscany or
a trendy new shade of orange.
Death is flipping pages, stacking
coffee cups, handing out hauntings
of those blue slippers. Such flimsy
reassurance, faith creased like
a paper airplane, a momentary flight.

When I'm called into the false
cheeriness of post-op, my
first sight is your bare feet, a hint
of blue stain on your left heel.
How insistent feet can be,
your big toe gnarled and aggressive,
the spaces between your tendons
like trenches in a battlefield.
Now that your ankles are back
in action, your shoulder bandage
barely resembles a big scare.
Your father shuffles off to supper.
Cancer, schmancer. Wheelies down the hall.
My heart can take a break, return
to being just a plain old hammer.

88 DECEMBERS

December well on its way to being
subsumed: tree up, bedecked, strewn
crèche, a chorus line of Christmas cards
across the mantelpiece. There's my father
still sitting on the sofa, watching
reruns of *Lawrence Welk*,
an accordion version of "Silent Night."

If you keep your eyes on him, you'll
notice he's dying, blood in the corners
of his mouth, gifts with his name on them
slowly sagging open, a dent
in the cushion suddenly all that's left
of 88 Decembers. It's been 4 years now
but he keeps disappearing on cue,
a new holiday ritual.
This year we've left out the tree,
hoping to mislead memory.

No, there he is, stubborn bloodstain,
stinking of pine and that scorched
smell of bulbs. What can I do
but fake busy like all the other elves
at the mall, try to find my wife
the skirt of her dreams,
track down my former best friend
and bring him back to the way
it should have been, find myself
something deep to hold me.

Longing in the place of everything
else. Aching from the ankles up,
I haunt the sales racks, comparing
needs to costs, looking for
a wholeness that won't get lost.

GET LOST

He's ironing his cool shirt,
the black one with sleek ivory stripes,
when his right wrist begins to shake.
Just a slip and he'd be scalded,
but that's not it, the crisis
is in amongst the muddled nerves,
hormones flashing at tear ducts
like toy ambulances. What's this
all about? The alarm clock of loss
went off before 6, surely he's
accrued some stealth, some heft, since then.
But loss it is, one hair too many
blown from his head, one great idea
sledding for a dark-ice end, a word
left dangling at the slam of
every sentence. It's not the done
deals that palsy him, the buried
parents, the scraps of youth, the old
collection of Beatles' cards
that vanished into someone else's
greed. No, the old griefs are slowly
arching into figurines, dust
collectors. It's this very moment
that's suddenly quaking, stirring up
distances too wide to cost, too
willful to calm. Bon voyage, good
riddance, get lost. His wedding ring
flies off his finger, an instant
UFO. Your love for him
spins inside out, a shrug of broken
bones. Someone not even born yet
shouts *No!*, her open mouth a begging
bowl. Shakes intensifying into
shivers, the iron hissing
in his hand, his shirt looking flat
and skinned. He'll lose this shirt one day,

time's dependable fray, which makes
him love it just a little less.
He'll lose the stripes, the pearly buttons,
the way the collar likes to strut.
Lose the hot cool,
the way the cotton adds his nakedness
to its list of accomplishments.

DOUBLE 2: PERFECT STRANGER

Ages ago you thought he was your father,
skinny knob of a man robbing
doorways of their emptiness, making

floorboards cry. But no way Dad
would just hang around, not without
his portable fireplace of a pipe, not

when his grave, lying on top of your mother,
is so damn comfy. This was a stranger,
according to the warning bells in your brain,

someone who had wandered in
on a tight-ass freeze-up of a day
and found corners to his liking, lots of

books on which to prop his head,
lace curtains to tangle the sunlight
into safety nets. Could he be

the brother you never found, or
the friend you didn't take the time to make?
Or the lover you've tiptoed around for years

careful not to wake? Who is this
figure on your couch, shape behind
your shower curtain, shadow

at the bottom of your basement stairs?
On shaky days, you wonder if he might be deadly,
a waste of patience, breath clenching itself in the closet.

So much life between you, a spill of
dimensions, an overcrowding of realities.
What if *he* and *here* are simply compliments,

coincidences that have no other stories?
You live with someone who makes no sense,
now there's a haunting, a French existentialist

of a ghost. You've started wishing him sweet
dreams when he floats to the foot of your bed.
Perfect stranger, even after all these years.

RAPTURE

1/

Liftoff. A pair of black and white sneakers left behind in the mud, a squelch on its way to extinction, sinners writhing with the dinosaurs. The Christians call it *Rapture*, underpants strewn across emptiness, no need for modesty anymore. God summons and everyone leaps, jerry-built skin and bones. Do the dogs go with us, the Jehovah Witnesses, the keepsakes that holy-up the mantelpiece? Our future love for each other, can we string it across our groins and still be innocent? But wait, if all this had already happened 30 years ago, there'd be no need for us, or that mountain ash feeding the robins, or the entire Tarantino oeuvre, or the zip zip of the internet. What was left of the world would have caved in, all that anchored evil.

2/

What would it feel like to be sucked out of our shoes, to know that earthly things like coffee cups and hardcover novels are nothing more than props dropped loudly on a stage? In the middle of a thought, stop and think about such loss. The wind and its power grip, *up* every bit as easy as falling down had always been. A side-swipe of eagle, a feathery fist, or maybe a jet, the faithless with their screams stuck to the windows. Oh, how the frightened kids in us believed, every little breeze, kaboom! The scathing friction of being stripped mid-air, speed burns everywhere, socks and shirts billowing like sin-parachutes.

DRIVE 2: RISK

A drill of highway dodging
on her way to the specialist,
her immune system steeling itself
for that tissue paper gown
and all those questions.
Just her eyes and wrists that are
driving, with occasional backup
from her neck. Not used to these
city speeds and weaves, she sometimes
doesn't check her blind spot
until mid-lane change, trusting to a half-
assed toss of fate. Is the sick part
of her a potential suicide?
The courage of the hopeless, tin
drummers marching into cannonballs.
Is there only time to do
or die, veer towards the exit sign
like an unprepared Girl Guide?

The doctor's office: a jammed freeway
of pill bottles, files on the verge
of exploding and gold-framed
positive thoughts. Swerving around
the worst of her symptoms, she steers
suffering into a long sentence
with at least three overpowering
verbs. She's still here, playing pin-
the-tail on the diagnosis,
practicing how to take a chance.
Until the little doom in her
back pocket says, *Aargh!*, and leaps out
onto the desk. Slam, the doctor
dazzles with the flat of his hand,
squashes the son of a bitch. No
untreated symptoms, no Russian
roulette. A prescription pad
bordered with bloodstained daisies.

Home again, a sigh, highways
cheated of their crash
for another day. Yet
the risks are still inside
her, genetics and its trick poodles,
its stack of ribbon-covered hoops.
She could self-destruct at any
moment, miss a crucial stair,
swallow a handful, neglect to
take another breath. Look at those
pink tulips on the kitchen table,
opening so wide their petals
are dropping off. Is there such
a thing as being too alive?
Surviving is dangerous,
exposed to all those clock-punched ghosts.
Speeding down the brainway, each
new resolve the death of a lesser thought.

AS LUCK WOULD HAVE IT

I press the button, take my ticket,
proceed into the Sunnybrook Hospital
parking lot, a simple procedure it would seem,
a few spins of the steering wheel,
empty space beckoning
like a slot in a pinball machine.
As luck would have it, I'm not the one
with cancer, with brazen red scalpel scars
and a drainage tube protruding from what
used to be mystery. I'm the one
providing the car, the designated driver,
searching for a space that doesn't seem to exist.
The place is packed, walls of fenders
and dead headlights holding me back.
My friend will think yet another luck
has abandoned him, consider calling a cab.
He'll have to put on his own socks,
despite being told not to bend.
In the end, he'll get philosophical, measure
all the levels of aloneness, decide that this one
is more of a bubble than a grave,
sit down and wait for the pop.
Meanwhile, my upper lip is sweating, every
round a wow of failure. I've even honked the horn,
hoping to jump-start some compact, chase it
to the nearest *Exit* bleed. Or should I just stop here,
middle of the lane, leap clear, a rescue mission,
pray that fate not tow me away, that my inner
Harrison Ford suddenly springs to action
like an inflatable doll? What a surprise,
my pus-stained friend gathered in my arms
and sped to freedom, the wind of it all
blowing through the holes where his nodes used to be.
If only fantasy could heal, if only cars
could grow huge, feathery wings. I drive and drive
until a gap finally appears, a puff of exhaust.

I'm coming, I'm almost here.
In a sixth floor room, my friend listens
for the B-flat of the elevator's beep,
four walls on the verge of collapsing,
a miraculous faith in parking spots.

PLYMOUTH SUNDANCE

Four years past his death, I'm finally
letting go of my father's car,
lemon to end all lemons. It sat
in the driveway these last two years, a red
reminder of how emptiness creates such space,
how a shrunken old man was replaced
by a hulk of rust and gleam.
No-one complained that one
state was less than another. It stood
against the elements, the neglect.
Night after night, tires sinking
into asphalt like dinosaur bones.
The only trouble was when the brakes
seized as it was being towed out
into the street. But that could be fixed
with a few harsh bangs. *Good as new*,
the next owner will claim, knowing
nothing about the past.

Bought when he was eighty,
this was my father's first new car.
My mother had forgotten who
she was and had lost the right
to a thrifty opinion. He slipped out
to the dealership alone, not
wanting me to see him agree
to everything: the rustproofing,
the various fleecings, the extended
warranty. But then he drove directly
to my house, showing off the fold-down
back seat and the air conditioning
at the flick of a button. Toyota
fan myself, I wrinkled my nose
like some gruesome *Bewitched* impression
and forced him to beg me
to take the wheel. Driving

around the block, meanly empowered,
morphing into Captain Intolerance.
We both knew a car was never just
a car, Freud and son. I called him gullible,
a wrench blow right between his eyes.

When I wrote the cheque for my used
Camry, I forgot for a moment
how to spell my last name. Power
locks, power speakers, rooftop window,
all those toys. *Something else
to go wrong*, I heard him say
when I rolled home and parked beside
the Sundance. But I wouldn't let him
see me twitch. The trick isn't
knowing anything, but acting it out
in convincing little scenes.
Maybe I should stick to cabs, or
simply walk away. Now that he's
finally gone, I can't even ask
him what's always going wrong.
Instead, I'll continue driving
into distances as if they were
red stars on a map.

MOSQUITO CONTROL

All morning, the shiver-thud
of helicopter, small town
skies carved into belittlement.
How fragile our bucolic charms,
collapsing at the first snort
of a roar. *The Bulletin*
refers to it as mosquito
control; we think
of it as pure poisoning.
The piglet-shaped clouds are dropping
pellets on the baby wheat
and the always milky cows,
trickling down our chimneys,
wreaking havoc on anything even
resembling an egg. Screwing with
the sex life of winged tormentors
as if Lucifer himself had
gone into the serial killing
business, no more angel spawn.
Later, when skies have softened
and the helicopter sits in a field
like a headbanging dragonfly,
we drive the country roads searching
for signs of death. Are those bare trees
busy tugging at their buds,
or are they choking on lethal
gulps? And that mushed
rabbit in the vetch, two tons
of tire or a big deep breath?
Are those pellets or bulrush fluff?
They say ditches are where
the chemistry is really
hopping, larvae too small to see
shrivelling into Hiroshimas.
And to think, once upon a time
we'd have laid lovers down here, sucked

grass that would cast green shadows
on their unsuspecting necks.
Are you ready? squeals the twenty-
foot sign outside the Baptist church.
Hell, no, one breath leads to another,
as much theology as we need to get by.
But that's just us, our doomsday
scenes, our cravings for intensity.
Mostly, we prefer our demise
to remain unseen, tinier
than fleas, invisible as
angels. The buzz in our heads
is mosquito-like, but that can't be,
we've offed the little bastards,
we're free, we're terminally free.

SAY SO

The dead have nothing to do but advise,
that should be the slogan hanging over
cemetery gates, an invitation to kick off
your shoes and wade in amongst
the tombstones, all those expiry dates,
find yourself a cozy name or appealing statue
and start spilling beans: fractured hearts,
unrequited gains, bad scenes knocking you
adrift. Spell it out, use big words like
acrimony and *irreversible*, but don't neglect
the crawly details that can twist jealousy
into rage: the lipstick blur, the mysterious
VISA bill. Tell the truth – if it feels like
an ice pick, say so; if it screams, scream.
Sit there on the lush, well-fertilized lawn
and explain everything: the ooze
of your teardrops, the peel of your dreams
coming undone. When you're finished,
sum it up, ask for guidance, specifics, names
and numbers. You deserve all the proof
you can find: fingerprints, ticket stubs, soiled
underthings. Take a good, long look
and then sit back and listen. The dead have
silences to say. Have you ever heard such balance?
Nothing lost, nothing over, nothing pondered, nothing
feared. Just your voice bouncing off a slab of stone,
just the facts that can never be changed,
just the glorious emptiness of here.

HEAVEN-BENT

We line up in the blurry rain
outside the cemetery gates,
a list of griefs, engines idling,
funeral flags faltering
from our antennae. Suddenly,
a break in traffic, the processional
proceeds, the grit of gravel
doing its rubber crunches,
the truth edging closer to that
blank hole we call fact.

When it's over and the rain
has flipped to a Scotch mist,
we note how little there is
to remember, as if the afternoon
had been buried beside the body.
Perhaps one red rose
will stand out for its woundedness.
And that felt-like fake grass
that the casket rolls over,
strangely haunting. Oh,
and a cloud or two, heaven-bent.

Only a few of us really knew
the departed, so we stretch
into our euphemisms
like slip-sliding shoes, stick
comments about the blessings
of memory into appropriate slots.
Then we head home, stunned
that so far we're still getting away
with it. Our black jackets float
a sour smell of mud, but nothing
that a good dry cleaning won't abolish.

Why so grim, it's all natural,
the decay at the core of every
joy, the gristle beneath a boy's
soft skin. Pleasure the moment,
whatever ways we can. Tonight,
at the Easter party, some of us
will finally don the cotton rabbit's ears,
fearless of appearing silly, raise
our pale fists into paws,
gnaw on imaginary leaves of air.

GIVING AWAY THE GARDEN

for Sharon Wilston

Heel on the shoulder of the shovel,
followed by the kind of pressure
it would take to break a neck,
again, again, until the dirt has been
thoroughly entered, a circle of slices,
the plant – toad lily or black
knight delphinium or nameless clematis –
ready to wrangle and rise, roots clinging
to clumps of the familiar, a strategic embrace.

Generosity, sharing her garden
the way lesser creatures swap spit.
A bag of hen and chickens sits waiting
for the drive to someone else's mini-Eden.
A sprinkle of lime, a gush of water, the least
one can do. No matter that the unearthed
princess rose draws a bead of blood; it's natural
to resist, to want to hold the status quo
to your stem like an intoxicating scent.

She won't be daunted, handing over buds
and shoots, brimming with Latin names and
rules for care. This one, you breathe on
twice a day, and that, you sing to
in a small grey voice, the way a rain cloud
would if it wasn't such a soggy wreck.
At times, it looks like she's offering
her own thin hands, wispy tendrils
creating their own trellises of reach and touch.

And when she offers thin air, take it,
the possibilities will be more majestic
than colours you can actually see.
Plant it close to you, semi-shadow,
but don't be surprised when it starts
to tower, a magic beanstalk of non-stop
desire. She knows you've never really
grown out of the mad faith stage
and would love to wear a flower for a face.

DEVIL DEATH

You have an idea now of what the devil looks like
when he's breaking hearts: a rapturous, rolled eyeball's glaze,

cheeks swollen to plums, just a pink bit of tongue hanging out.
He isn't really there, he'll claim, transported by his

addiction to causing pain, off in some evil vestry
counting the drops of blood he's managed to squeeze

from your total devotion. He's burning strands of your hair,
a soft stink reminding you of how *mortal* and *dead*

mean the same thing. Pieces of your love, such strange
dismemberment, a toe climbing across his shoulder blade,

a chin buried in his belly, and sweat, streams of what
used to be your grip pouring down his spine, making it

impossible to climb back up. You have been struck,
offed, deracinated, every slant of shame you've ever

trembled. No need for future wariness, the worst
has already happened. It's up to you whether

you shrivel into a garlic bud or splay your limbs
on the nearest oak, a do-or-die new attitude.

You can finally join the French Foreign Legion
now that there's room for a camel in your chest.

You can even take a course on devilry:
how to become him in seven stumbling steps.

Or you can copycat the Buddhists and stoke compassion,
the loneliness at the heart of so much hate.

Whatever. The rest of your life is rising
in tiny, god-like ways. To stop and drown in lilacs

or pinch a clothespin on your nose? It's not the devil's
choice anymore, he's already spit and swallowed.

The little that's left of you is back in charge:
a middle finger, a taste bud, a brave idea.

FIX ME

>   for Emilio Aceti

He says *catastrophe*, what we all need
in order to reassess our lives.
His fingers are up my kitchen light socket
as he speaks, eureka, his spine
one spark away from a lit Christmas tree.
I've always admired handymen, their
doable lingo, their fearlessness
in the face of deconstruction. Lose a leg
and learn to hop, the best damn hopper
in the land. Fall apart and put yourself
back together, tighter, with more tilt.
He wields his Phillips like a magic wand:
let there be shock upon shock.

He wants to fix me, up to his wrist
in my messy chest, tapping, turning.
If only my heart could be properly tamped,
a few illusions siphoned out. Or
a strut replaced, some ballast, maybe
an extra screw or two. He wants me
functioning, happiness engaged in its
piston push and pull. And while he's at it,
give my brain a thorough scrape, wire brush
the spark plugs, oil the blades, get some
power thoughts flowing through. It wouldn't be
the worst thing if I tumbled down the back stairs,
rearranged some vrooms. Here, put my finger
in the socket, salvation's bright kaboom.

He leaves discouraged at how depression
clings, phones later to let me know
he isn't giving up, even if it
takes a nail gun or a Nazi
pair of pliers. His tenacity

is all I can think of as I stand
for hours in the kitchen, flicking
the fixed light on and off. Light and dark,
or is it dark and light? Which way's which
has always been a fumble, me with my
two left hands. It's all a matter of
perception, whether I'm losing or
surrendering to grace, dying or
learning how to live again. Later,
I'll hold a new light bulb between my palms
like a phoenix egg, twist it into flame.

TULIPS

The dead have plotted tulips
around the cemetery gates,
slathered them in bright colours
so they might seduce you.
Today they're in luck, some high

school kid killed in a drunken
skid, a bevy of underage
mourners making black look cute,
hanging out amidst the flower-
beds, dying to wrench some blooms

from the cold earth to wear them
in their hair. The dead would like
to see them dance, a mating
ritual; you'd be surprised
at the amount of naked flesh

they catch on summer nights.
But it's been a long, monotonous
winter, and everyone is
anxious for a little tulip
blood, bones slithering on top

of bones. *Come in*, a chorus
of the dead urge, *enter*. So
many further delights inside.
You can watch the boy's coffin
shimmy from side to side

as it's lowered into
the luscious dark. You can kneel
down with the four-leaf clovers
and watch him land. Or you can
flip over on your back, become

the clover, the whole damn lawn,
peering up the skirts of all
those adolescent girls
who think that endings are most
beautiful when desire wears a scar.

What else is a spring bulb
but reincarnation? The dead
have planted themselves, clever
narcissists, and are steaming
to be plucked. Place your fingers

around a tulip's swell
and draw that grasp down to
the knotty edge of root and dirt,
then pull with all your might,
unearth the bugger, wave it

in the air, a boisterous
claim to another victory,
another day above the dust.
Look, the young mourners are all
crying, susceptible to

anything that pretends to be
the end. Shouldn't you go
rescue a few before the dead
start stroking their ankles,
slowly drawing them down?

YOU ARE SURROUNDED BY MUSIC

You are surrounded by music,
the hospital bed wedged
between shelves of CDs,
the stereo always playing,
quiet pop from Jolie Holland
and Phil Collins, and the faster
stuff, Fountains of Wayne,
huffing on about summer romance.
Hardly any gravity
in the air, even the heartbreak songs
sliding on slippery guitars,
leaving you the lyric no-one dares,
the gaunt verse about abandonment.
You're wearing a T-shirt
announcing *Cancer Sucks*,
yet your spine a tumour tree,
what a fright of horror, something
Lou Reed would drone about.
But it's Norah Jones in the next tray,
mellow little plum, promising
to come next time the right voice calls.
Is it possible for something so weightless
to have a double meaning? Is Norah
flirting with death, a bone coquette?
Are the Wayne boys madly in love
with ghosts or is everyone who enters
this room suddenly slowly dying?

BONFIRE

The neighbours are burning again tonight,
heaps of what used to be a tree, sunset
clouds hanging low on the horizon
as if full of blood. They are burning
what they no longer need – yesterday's
news balled into paper bombs,
weather reports of rain tomorrow,
those pesky worries that when saved
and sorted can ruin entire lives.

A stack of pornography curling in on itself
like an ancient engraving of Hell.
They are burning the gods who have
disappointed them, the lack of gods
for whom stubbornness is an art.
The night is leaping with heat, flickering
the way death does when it rubs
against energy. Night sweating,
cinders trickling down columns of

darkness. *Pop*, a low note, like
sap imploding. Blinded, they stumble,
shedding their inconsequential selves –
buttons and bones, cinnamon hearts,
crisp cotton collars – leaving nothing
but a ring of blackened stones,
hopes so dense and heavy
they're incapable of bursting
into anything as capricious as flames.

CONCERT HALL, THE CARLU

Billie Holiday played here, once upon a time,
a glistening gardenia in her hair
whiter than spotlights, than the glint
of her teeth as they sharpened the low notes,
than the band's Saturday night/Sunday morning
shirts. She toned misery pure, something
scrubbed to its beams. A crystal
candy dish filled with happy sugar,
then the sizzle of a teardrop.
Billie cried on this very stage, joyous
emanations, so glad to be the brunt.

No place feels roomy anymore, all
the ghosts, both strangers and your own private
entourage. Who's that up there with Billie,
your brazen aunt, the one who sent back steaks
a certain shade of pink? Or just some ancient doll,
silver-rinsed, with the stale smell of men
still sticking to her fingertips. The crowd
isn't here to listen, but to haunt. *You wanna
see broken*. Lady Day and the Heartaches,
New York City thick. Imagine chorus
lines and corpses in the same blurred frame.

When no-one's looking, you sneak on stage, try to
pass as someone so far gone you're nothing but
a cloud of sobbed perfume. *Hey, Lady*.
The melody is easiest, the smoky slurs,
the downbeats that smudge even the brightest lips.
If only someone could take a picture,
peel back the loss. You and Billie stoned
to the collarbones, those useless little wings,
shoulders most of the way to a slump. Oh, God,
the lights are actually supporting you,
such brilliant scaffolds, all the ruin propped inside.
It's always been hard to stay involved and so

you sidle to a corner, give Billie back
the white lie of flower and gown, the faithlessness
of highs. As long as she keeps crooning, death will
be okay, the audience relinquishing their faults.
Truth be told, we're all unhappy, cold black coffee
pouring through our veins. No need to hype it,
to rush headlong into nothingness, not when
Billie has so much more suffering to cover,
so many blanched pools in which to bury
this and every other goddamned night.

PERENNIAL

Shopping for perennials, nonplussed:
wishing he could try them on, colour coordinate,
match texture with breadth. He loves
a hosta's sprawl, but these starters
are substantially puny, liable to
moon a little and then, lopsided, fold
limply in the dirt. Maybe an astilbe
would be better, feather in a cap,
or a blue delphinium, pomp squared.
A coral bell with its soft chimes
or an evening primrose with its daubs
of butter. He can't take his eyes off
the spiderwort's Martha Graham hands.
The challenges of emptiness,
a penchant for that God-thing: creating
energy from little puffs of dust.

And so he buys and digs and floods
the roots with swirls of muddy water,
graves, he thinks, and wonders why
creation wasn't tempted by the symmetry –
nursery and cemetery sharing the same trench,
the way tulips shoot up only to be shot down,
disappearing back into their bulbs
like moles diving for cover
at the first struck match of dawn.
Hard not to feel lofty, even arrogant:
up with coral bells, down with delphies,
deciding what shape this spill will take,
what colours will drain his face
as he bends down to worship.
He even plants a thumb or two, some drops
of sweat, a naughty thought of you,
hoping for a glossy garden spread,
a lavish *paradisio*.

Fast forward, here they are, man and
masterpiece, as perennial as
mortality gets. He still has his flourishes,
but spends most of his time plucking
clover and bindweed, dickering
over mulch and moisture, thinning out,
cutting back. A long time since he last
wrote a poem about the colour pink
constantly interrupting him with its
luscious winks. Long time since he's
glided outside in the middle of the night
to drink the dew from a hosta leaf.

THURSDAY CRUEL

A pretty woman spit from the side window
of a black car today, and, on Eglinton,
a high-rise was being demolished,
a giant wedding cake kicked in. You kept
seeing things you didn't want to see. The sky,
for example, a cringe of grey, like laundry

still dirty, hung on a line. The month of
August splayed in the gutter, hardly more
than a squirm. A future was on its way
and it wouldn't be nice, morning glories
shrivelling on a twisted vine, a breeze
picking up enough heft and trash

to qualify as bluster. And you, the stranger
in the passing lane, fighting a quibble of
nausea, a certainty that something simply
wasn't right. Could it be that adding up the days
had finally snatched its toll and rolled
that tombstone back in place? Or was this

a general malaise, headlines snipped
from daily papers and pasted psycho-like
on a blank page? Maybe Israel had gone
too far this time, maybe that baby carriage
outside the Science Centre was a bomb,
maybe the stick man stumbling from the 7-Eleven

was dying rather than drunk. You wouldn't be
surprised. After all, a woman spit today,
hit the breeze with a lippy punch and let fly,
almost finished off the collapsing high-rise.
She made you want her there and then,
so you could cry together or you could stroke

her chin, feel something other than lost.
Thursday, August 24 will go down as cruel,
a day holding its stomach. Not a kiss
in sight, not a bit of summer light. Just a case
of nerves, a twist of expectations, as if
your gaze had found a way to make a fist.

BUILDING STAIRS

for Mike Gall

I can't do it, can't keep the jigsaw straight,
can't rip a plank, can't tell a riser from a tread.
And yet I'm helping build stairs, pretending
that up and down are simple acts. *Bring me
a four-by-four*, he says. *Bring me a square*.
I wave tools in the air like products
on *The Price is Right*, already distracted
by a cluster of winged ants swarming
over the remnants of a board. Who's the biggest
miracle – Mike the master, or Mother Nature
with her stair-defying dazzle, or the fact
that I've come so far on such little skill?
The measuring tape keeps snapping back,
the nails duck my hammer, the cut line veers.
Imagine God slaving six days, building ladders
and calling them waterfalls and trees, creating
something never seen before. The world takes shape
an inch at a time – Adam the finger, the wrist,
the climb to collarbone. A staircase ascending
from the insolent sand, becoming air, becoming sky.
Mike's head appears from a sawdust cloud, reminding me
that once upon a time the moon was just an idea.
Despite my clumsiness, my godlessness,
faith rises, heart lifted rib by rib.

THE MAPLES ARE BLEEDING

The maples are bleeding, slowly
draining death's fluster
where sap and shade are temporary
distractions, where bareness is more
than just transition: a way of being
alone. Today, you feel sick,
cheeks flushed like squashed apples.
Loving badly in the midst of it all,
your heart sucking itself thin, trying
to conserve what little energy is left.
Why, in the quiet moments, is dying
so nimble? You prefer the thick
of things, the pudding of August heat.
Curse this October frailty, these
crimson stains that turn the wind
into a killer. *Indian summer,*
a pretty way of undermining fever.
Hey, deadly, I see you peeking
through what soon will be
empty space. You're moving
your sickness out to the backyard,
looking for something raw and ready
to fall. Hand you a rake and
suddenly you're a gravedigger.
It's that simple, a breath broken
free from its swinging branch.

WHERE DOES IT HURT?

Where does it hurt? In the thighs
where I crouched on the roof
throwing down leaves the trees
had tossed away. Through my
shoulders where shovels and rakes
had done some tidying up.
My right thumb and its demanding
sidekick mouse. My left ear
where the phone pummelled
all those voices into one shrill scream.
Just being alive is a major pain.
Knees and elbows, those marching drums.
And the spine, ladder to forgetfulness,
abandoned feet on every rung.

Then there's inner suffering –
the sputtering wires beneath
the gaily painted drywall,
My appendix, shouting to be
let out. The sore hole where my
gallbladder used to be. Kinks
and outright blockages. Something
like a sciatic nerve upgrading
my hip to a hot spot. One hair
near the top of my head writhing,
like one bad thought ruining
the entire story. An ache
behind my better eye, vision
crushed to a blue fist.

At the core, the love place
where hurt shot its first curse. It's not
my balls after all, at best a sting
as I swing to avoid collision
with an amorous knee.
Or my cock, throbbing but happy,

too dumb to malinger. That just
leaves my heart, predictable
little scrape and scorch, the source
with a skewer for a flagpole, its
countless perforations. Love me/
leave me, in that order, of course.
Oh, how it pains, as if it had
fallen from a roof; drummed and raked,

as if it had been trained to break.

THE WHOLE OF IT

The dark is a door slamming, no
subtlety about it, a tantrum.
So much anger pursuing us, escapees
from paradise, still paying for our fathers'
faults. We might as well sin for
ourselves, earn the derision.
One man drinks, another tosses
desire on its broken back.
The shame feels good
when the dark takes away everything else.

The cold is a stone wall, a shoulder
banging its frailty against the impossible.
And we think *gasp* is just another
word for breathe. Nature striving
to put an end to us: mountain rages
and frozen declarations of waves.
Instead of dying, we bundle
our tenacity in shivers, outlast
the gusts and screams.

The loss is a hole cut out
from under us, a cartoon blade.
Anything we fear will probably happen.
Hope, for example, an evil gnome.
We put on speed and desperation,
crashing through inner space.
Not even love, garbled
and spat, makes any sense.

The whole of it is a chimney going up
in flames, darkness cloning itself
with glee. So much depends
on destroying us, making room
for the next batch, the devolution of faith
into schemes. All we can do is die
in droves, see how many of us fall from grace
on the same day. The entire sky
on fire this time, a vengefulness, ravens
hanging upside down from blood-scorched trees.

EVERYTHING IS GOING TO BE FINE

or so they tell us, the experts
adjusting their skirts on *Oprah*,
the Buddhists who have revealed
a path to the self-help shelves,
the therapists pretending that mystery
is simply another name for unexplored.
We get over it eventually,
little timers lodged in our
cracked hearts. The perfect moment
to scurry on with our lives –
new day, new day.

But then there's Al Gore, glaciers
melting all over his face.
And the Billy Graham clones
with their Christmas lists of sinners.
Not to mention the former lover
whose leaving town in the middle of the night
was like pasting a band-aid
on a severed body part. Jesus,
some of us actually die, don't we?
No matter how hard we try – like
Cathy and her stacks and stacks of faith,
lying in an urn in a wall in a cemetery,
a world where only losers give up.

Grief took us as far as it could
and left us here. We wander
face to face all day long,
eyes averted, acting self-contained.
It's only when we think we're alone
that we slip off our happy chains
and listen to the stats man state
everything is not okay.
Floods and flames and bombs
buried in the flesh, thefts and cheats

and failed getaways. Oh, yes,
there's another side to this,
a bloat of second chances,
all our drastics floating past
like untethered prayers.

DEATH DATE

    for Cathy Stanley 1956–2006

We put you in a wall, death date
sunk in grey stone, the Beatles
on the boom box singing "Let It Be"
as if we had a choice. It's a long song,
giving us plenty of time to stare
at your name, the one piece of you
that feels abandoned as well as left behind.
And the view, your view
if ashes could actually see:
a birch tree on a slope, a bevy of
tombstones, a few black squirrels
putting on a show for peanuts.
On the other side of the wall – the cheap
seats – you'd have looked out on traffic
all day, an eternity of destination envy.
Better the birch, the kingly squirrel tails,
and at night, the darkness that surpasses
a simple lack of light, another kind of wall.

Miles away, on a different road,
trying to get used to distance,
I catch sight of a red-tailed hawk
in a gnarled ironwood. Would you think
bird or *angel*? All I know for sure
is that you'd be pleased and so I spin
the car around, go back for a second look.
Is this a glimpse of your rareness, your
ability to charge the air around you?
The hawk sees me in a way I've not been
seen before and flings its wings
from the grey branch, lifting the very idea
of death into a bloody flourish of freedom,
tail feathers burning up the air.
Who cares where it disappears – the field

it left behind is simmering with after-
presence, ripples of energy that crease
my eyes, spill a little blue all over the day.

As long as I remember that death
is a new relationship, not a gaping hole,
I will walk the woods for you, drive
the highways, sing the undeniable songs.
At Maryholme, I show you how placid
Lake Simcoe can get on a mild November afternoon.
I read you the names of trees,
though without their leaves they look
surprisingly alike. Except the birches,
badges of ghostliness, how they make
every other bark resemble mist. Would you
believe me if I said I saw
that same cemetery squirrel scampering
across this grass, reminding me I stay
in one place no matter where I go? I think
you're probably the only one who believes me
as you pick up your long legs and dash
after the vision, leaving me alone
to name whatever else will come along.

ACKNOWLEDGEMENTS

The literary magazine is where the whole process of reaching out begins, a bridge built between reader and poet. I am deeply grateful to the following magazines and their hard-working editors for seeing something in these poems and giving them the opportunity to breathe…

Alien Sloth Sex, *All Rights Reserved*, *The Comstock Review*, *CV2*, *Dream Catcher*, *Existere*, *The Fiddlehead*, *Grain*, *Horsefly*, *The Literary Review*, *The Malahat Review*, *The New Quarterly*, *paperplates*, *Prairie Fire*, *PRECIPICe*, *Studio*, *Wascana Review* and *White Wall Review*.

A thousand thanks to Don McKay for the *joys of nit and pickdom*. His faith in my work is priceless, his ear impeccable. And to Karen Dempster whose support and love is essential to each and every word. A round of cheers to my three writing groups who weave in and out of all these lines. Hugs to the friends who make such a daily difference. Deep appreciation to those who appear throughout this book, both the losses and the gains.

Thank you to Noelle Allen and everyone at Wolsak & Wynn for the welcoming and the good work.

Barry Dempster was born in Toronto, Ontario, and educated in child psychology. He is the author of a novel, a children's book, two volumes of short stories and eleven collections of poetry. He has been nominated for the Governor General's Literary Award twice; for his first book, *Fables for Isolated Men*, and most recently for *The Burning Alphabet*, which won the Canadian Authors Association Chalmers Award for Poetry. From 1990 to 1997, he was Poetry and Reviews Editor for Poetry Canada. Presently, he is Senior Acquisitions Editor with Brick Books. In 2010, he was a finalist for the Ontario Premier's Award for Excellence in the Arts. He has been on the faculty at The Banff Centre as mentor for the Writing Studio, Wired Writing and Writing with Style programs; has conducted master classes all across the country and as far away as Chile; and has been the Writer-in-Residence at the Richmond Hill Public Library twice. He has read widely across Canada and in New York City. His most recent books include *Love Outlandish*, *Ivan's Birches* and *Blue Wherever*.